BPP Learning Media is grateful to the IASB for permission to reproduce extracts from the International Financial Reporting Standards including all International Accounting Standards, SIC and IFRIC Interpretations (the Standards). The Standards together with their accompanying documents are issued by:

The International Accounting Standards Board (IASB)
30 Cannon Street, London, EC4M 6XH, United Kingdom.
Email: info@ifrs.org Web: www.ifrs.org

Welcome to BPP Learning Media's AAT **Passcards for Advanced Bookkeeping.**

- They **save you time**. Important topics are summarised for you.
- They incorporate **diagrams** to kick-start your memory.
- They follow the overall **structure** of the BPP Course Book, but BPP Learning Media's AAT **Passcards** are not just a condensed book. Each card has been separately designed for clear presentation. Topics are self contained and can be grasped visually.
- AAT **Passcards** are **just the right size** for pockets and bags.
- AAT **Passcards focus on the assessment** you will be facing.
- AAT **Passcards focus on the essential points** that you need to know in the workplace, or when completing your assessment.

Run through the complete set of **Passcards** as often as you can during your final revision period. The day before the assessment, try to go through the **Passcards** again! You will then be well on your way to completing your assessment successfully.

**Good luck!**

For reference to the Bibliography of the AAT Advanced Bookkeeping Passcards please go to: www.bpp.com/learning-media/about/bibliographies

The BPP **Question Bank** contains activities and assessments that provide invaluable practice in the skills you need to complete this unit successfully.

## Notes

# 1: Bookkeeping transactions

## Topic List

- Purpose of an accounting system
- Books of prime entry
- Ledger accounts
- Elements of financial statements
- Principles of double entry bookkeeping
- Balancing off ledger accounts
- Sales tax
- The trial balance

*This chapter is an introductory chapter and serves to remind you of your Level 2 AAT accounting studies.*

*Key topics include the books of prime entry, double entry bookkeeping and balancing off ledger accounts.*

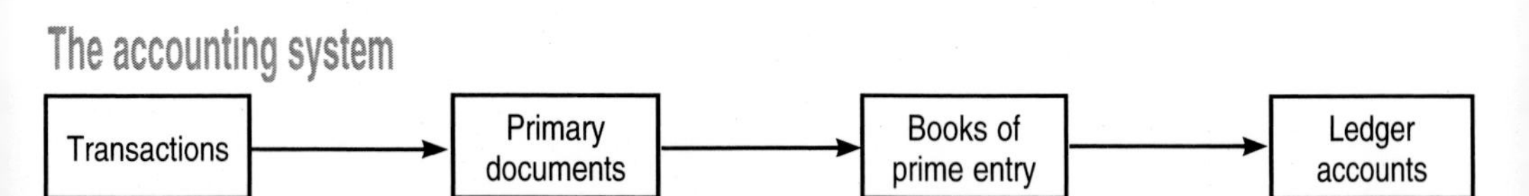


## Purpose of an accounting system

To ensure that all transactions are correctly recorded and can be gathered together for a period in order to prepare a set of financial statements

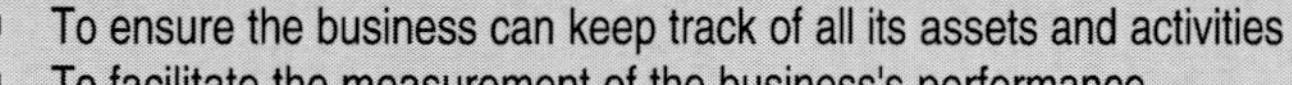

- To ensure the business can keep track of all its assets and activities
- To facilitate the measurement of the business's performance
- To help obtain financing and other forms of credit
- To meet statutory requirements

## The accounting system

Transactions → Primary documents → Books of prime entry → Ledger accounts

For each transaction there will be a primary document which is entered in a book of prime entry as the primary record.

| *Transactions* | *Primary document* | *Book of prime entry* |
|---|---|---|
| Cash sales | Receipt/till roll | Cash book – debit side |
| Credit sales | Sales invoice | Sales day book |
| Sales returns | Credit note | Sales returns day book |
| Receipts from credit customers | Remittance advice note | Cash book – debit side |
| Cash purchases | Cheque book stub/till receipt | Cash book – credit side |
| Credit purchases | Purchase invoice | Purchases day book |
| Purchases returns | Credit note from supplier | Purchases returns day book |
| Payments to credit suppliers | Cheque book stub/bank authorisation | Cash book – credit side |
| Other cash payments | Petty cash voucher | Petty cash book |
| Wages and salaries | Payroll records | Journal |

The totals and detail from each book of prime entry is transferred (posted) to the general ledger accounts using the principles of double entry bookkeeping.

## General ledger (main or nominal ledger)

Contains a separate ledger account for each type of income, expense, asset, liability and capital of a business

## Memorandum ledgers

**Do not** form part of the double entry bookkeeping system

### Sales ledger

Contains a ledger account for each individual receivable showing the amount owed by the customer and how it is made up

### Purchases ledger

Contains a ledger account for each individual payable showing the amount owed to the supplier and how it is made up

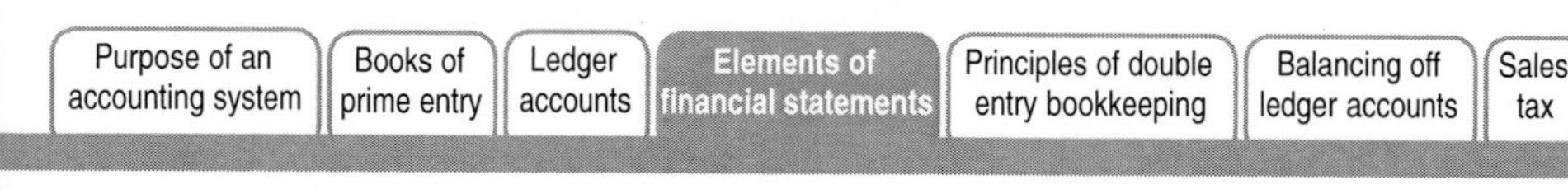


# Elements of financial statements

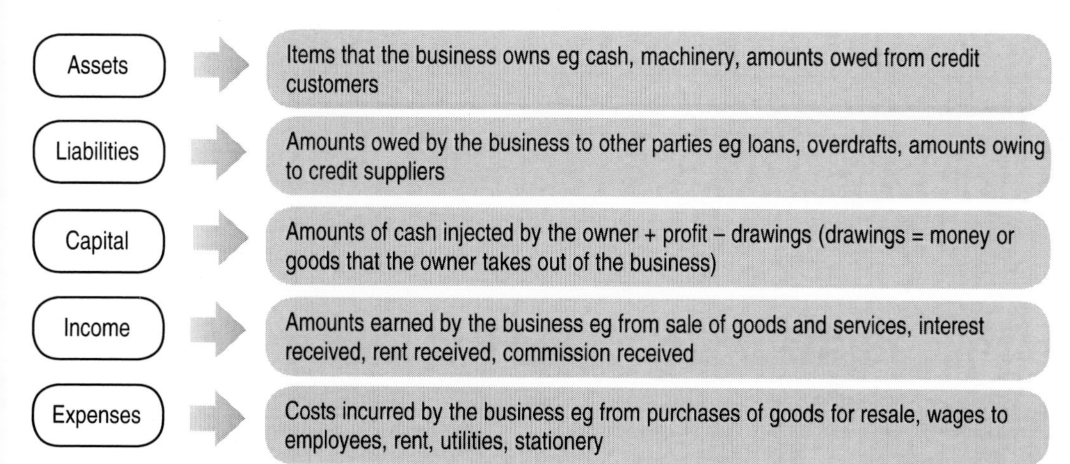

There are three main principles of double entry bookkeeping.

## Dual effect on business

Each transaction has two effects on the business eg the business buys goods for resale with cash – expenses (purchases) have increased and cash has decreased

## Separate entity concept

The owner of the business is separate from the business entity

## Double entry

Every transaction results in a debit and a credit

For example:

A business buys goods for resale in cash:

DR Purchases
CR Bank

or makes cash sales:

DR Bank
CR Sales

| D | **DEBIT**<br>Increases in |
|---|---|
| E | EXPENSES<br>eg advertising costs |
| A | ASSETS<br>eg new office equipment |
| D | DRAWINGS<br>eg the owner takes cash for his own use |
| | Decreases in liabilities, capital or income |
| | **Left hand side** |

| C | **CREDIT**<br>Increases in |
|---|---|
| L | LIABILITIES<br>eg amounts owed to suppliers for credit purchases |
| I | INCOME<br>eg make a sale |
| C | CAPITAL<br>eg owner puts money into the business |
| | Decreases in assets, drawings or expenses |
| | **Right hand side** |

# Balancing off ledger accounts

1. Add up the debit side and credit side separately
2. Put the larger of the two totals as the column total for both the debit and credit columns
3. Calculate the balancing figure on the side with the lower total
4. Describe the balancing figure as 'balance c/d' for a SOFP account or 'profit or loss account' for a SPL account
5. For SOFP accounts, show this balancing figure on the opposite side, below the totals line as the 'balance b/d'

**Note.** SOFP accounts are c/d and b/d each period; SPL accounts are transferred to the profit or loss account

## Examples of balancing off

### Bank (SOFP)

| | £ | | £ |
|---|---|---|---|
| Capital | 30,000 | Purchases | 800 |
| Sales | 400 | Rent and rates | 650 |
| | | Balance c/d | 28,950 |
| | 30,400 | | 30,400 |
| Balance b/d | 28,950 | | |

### Purchases (SPL)

| | £ | | £ |
|---|---|---|---|
| Bank | 800 | Profit or loss account | 1,250 |
| Purchases ledger control account | 450 | | |
| | 1,250 | | 1,250 |

**Sales tax**

Consumer tax imposed by government on certain goods and services (known as VAT in UK)

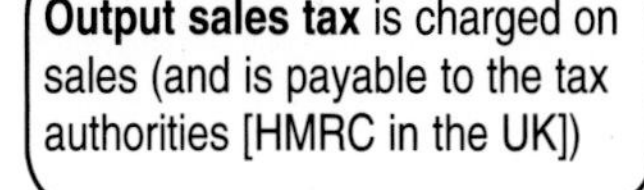

**Output sales tax** is charged on sales (and is payable to the tax authorities [HMRC in the UK])

**Input sales tax** is incurred on purchases (and is recoverable from the tax authorities [HMRC] if the business is VAT registered)

Settled net:

Output tax > input tax: difference paid to tax authority

Input tax > output tax: difference refunded by tax authority

## VAT Control account (SOFP)

| | £ | | £ |
|---|---|---|---|
| Bank (paid to HMRC) | 150 | Balance b/d | 150 |
| VAT on purchases (input tax) | 400 | VAT on sales (output tax) | 600 |
| Balance c/d | 200 | | |
| | 750 | | 750 |
| | | Balance b/d (owing to HMRC) | 200 |

**Trial balance** = List of all ledger account balances at the period end

At the period end, all ledger accounts are balanced off

The balances are listed in the trial balance which has separate columns for debits and credits

The total of the debit balances should equal the total of the credit balances (if not, there have been errors in the double entry)

## Trial balance at 31 December 20X2

| Account name | Debit £ | Credit £ |
|---|---|---|
| Bank | 28,950 | |
| Capital | | 30,000 |
| Purchases | 1,250 | |
| Rent | 500 | |
| Sales | | 1,550 |
| Rates | 150 | |
| Sales ledger control account | 1,150 | |
| Purchases ledger control account | | 450 |
| Totals | 32,000 | 32,000 |

Notes

# 2: Accounting Principles

## Topic List

- Financial statements
- Definitions of assets, liabilities, capital, income and expenses
- Accounting equation
- Organisational policies and procedures
- Ethical principles

*Having recapped the principles of double entry bookkeeping, this chapter takes us a stage further by looking at the definitions of assets, liabilities, capital, income and expenses in more detail and viewing them in the context of the accounting equation.*

*This chapter also outlines different types of organisational policies/procedures and their importance to the business. Then it examines the ethical principles which provide a framework for decisions made by accountants in their day to day work.*

You will not have to prepare financial statements. These have been included to help your understanding of assets, liabilities, capital, income and expenses.

**Statement of financial position**

| | £ |
|---|---|
| **ASSETS** | |
| **Non-current assets** | |
| Property, plant and equipment | 160,000 |
| Intangible assets | 20,000 |
| | 180,000 |
| **Current assets** | |
| Inventories | 35,000 |
| Trade and other receivables | 20,000 |
| Cash and cash equivalents | 15,000 |
| | 70,000 |
| **LIABILITIES** | |
| **Current liabilities** | |
| Bank overdraft | 16,000 |
| Trade and other payables | 34,000 |
| | 50,000 |
| **Net current assets** | 20,000 |
| **Net assets** | 200,000 |
| **CAPITAL** | |
| Capital | 180,000 |
| Add Profit for the year | 45,000 |
| Less Drawings | (25,000) |
| **Closing capital** | 200,000 |

**Statement of profit or loss**

| | £ |
|---|---|
| **Revenue** | 200,000 |
| **Less Cost of goods sold** | |
| Opening inventory | 40,000 |
| Purchases | 130,000 |
| Closing inventory | (50,000) |
| | (120,000) |
| **Gross profit** | 80,000 |
| Sundry income | 5,000 |
| Discounts received | 3,000 |
| | 88,000 |
| **Expenses** | |
| Rent and rates | 21,000 |
| Telephone | 3,000 |
| Electricity | 4,000 |
| Wages and salaries | 9,000 |
| Motor expenses | 5,000 |
| Discounts allowed | 1,000 |
| | (43,000) |
| **Profit** | 45,000 |

# Definitions of assets, liabilities and capital

**Statement of financial position**

Snapshot of business at one point in time (period end)

Shows what business owns (assets) and what it owes (liabilities)

Non-current assets

Assets held and used in business over the long term (> 1 year):

- Tangible assets: have physical substance (eg property, plant & equipment
- Intangible assets: no physical substance (eg licenses, brands)

Current assets

Assets used by business on a day-to-day basis (< 1 year) eg inventories, trade receivables and cash

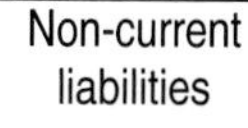

Long term debts of the business (> 1 year) eg bank loan

Current liabilities

Amounts owed by business due to day to day activities (< 1 year) eg trade payables, accruals, bank overdrafts and VAT liability to HMRC

Capital

Amounts contributed by the owner to the business plus profit less drawings (cash or goods withdrawn by the owner for personal use)

# Definitions of income and expenses

**Statement of profit or loss**

Summary of trading activities over a period of time (usually 12 months)

It shows amounts the business has earned (income) and costs that it has incurred (expenses)

Income – Expenses = Profit

## Examples of income:

- Sales
- Interest received
- Rental income

## Examples of expenses:

- Cost of goods sold
- Interest paid
- Gas and electricity
- Stationery
- Rent and rates

| | | |
|---|---|---|
| Debits | = | Credits |
| Assets | = | Liabilities + Capital |
| This can be rearranged: | | |
| **Assets – Liabilities** | **=** | **Capital** |
| Liabilities | = | Assets – Capital |

Your assessment might ask you to state the accounting equation (its most common format is: Assets – Liabilities = Capital) or to use it to find a missing figure.

To find a missing figure you might need to break down the different elements:

Assets = Non-current assets + Current assets

Liabilities = Non-current liabilities + Current liabilities

Capital = Opening capital + New capital introduced + Profit for the year – Drawings

Organisational policies and procedures are necessary because:

- Financial information is used by many stakeholders
- Information must be complete and accurate
- Policies and procedures must be in place to ensure the data is reliable

**Examples:**

- Authorisation of transactions
- Processing controls
- Physical controls
- Reviews of financial information
- Written record of procedures
- Segregation of duties

The AAT's *Code of Professional Ethics* applies to all members, including students.

The assessment is likely to focus on how ethical principles provide a guiding framework for an accountant's day-to-day work.

### Fundamental principles

- Integrity
- Objectivity
- Professional competence and due care
- Confidentiality
- Professional behaviour (AAT, 2014: p. 9)

### Threats to fundamental principles

- Self-interest
- Self-review
- Advocacy
- Familiarity
- Intimidation (AAT, 2014: p. 11)

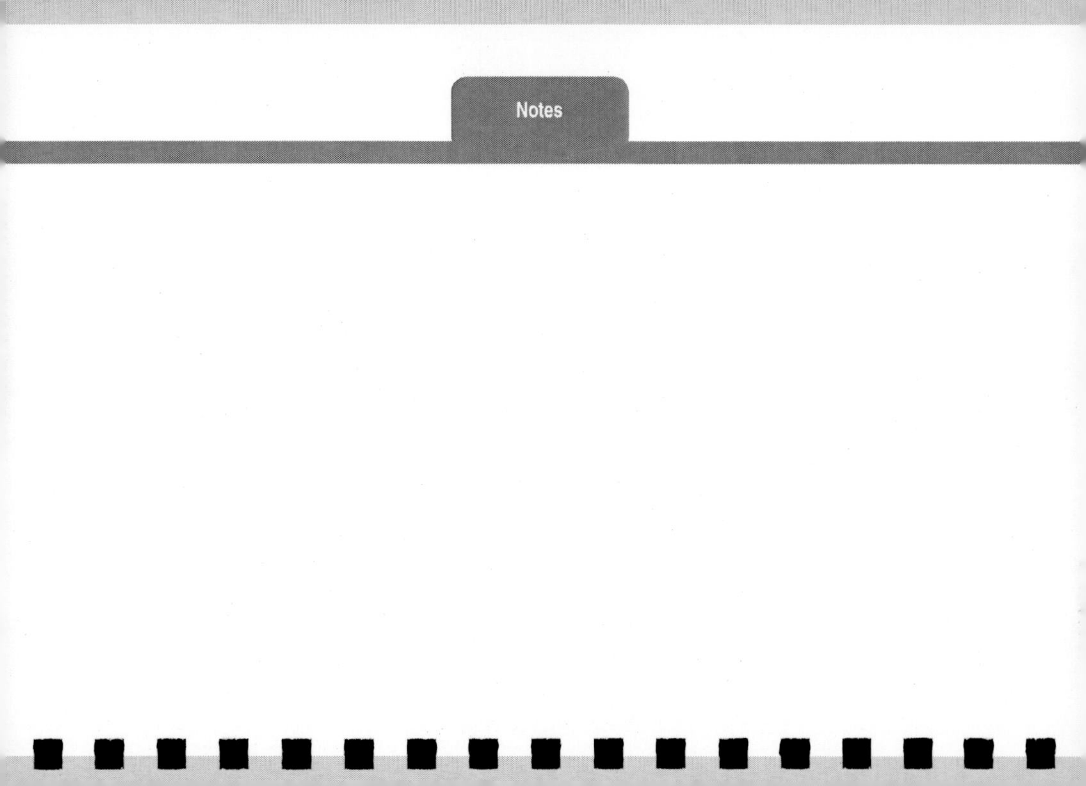
Notes

# 3: Purchase of non-current assets

## Topic List

- Capital v revenue
- Cost of non-current assets
- Authorising capital expenditure
- Methods of funding
- Double entry

*This is a very important chapter as non-current assets (covered in Chapters 3-5) are likely to feature heavily in the first two tasks of your assessment. The purchase of a non-current asset is often a significant cost and must therefore be accounted for appropriately.*

# Non-current assets: the basics

**Non-current asset**: acquired and retained within the business with a view to earning profits, normally used over more than one accounting period

## Examples

- Plant and machinery eg machine used in manufacturing
- Motor vehicles eg delivery vans, managers' cars
- Land and buildings eg building from which business operates
- Furniture and fittings
- Computer equipment

## Capital expenditure

Results in the acquisition, manufacture, replacement or improvement of non-current assets

## Revenue expenditure

For the trade of the business or to repair, maintain or service non-current assets

## Capitalisation Policy

- A minimum level of expenditure for items to be capitalised
- Items below this limit are recorded as an expense

Non-current assets should initially be recorded at **cost** which includes:

- Purchase price or construction costs
- Directly attributable costs to bring asset to location and condition necessary for operation eg
  - Initial delivery and handling costs
  - Installation and assembly costs
  - Costs of site preparation
  - Costs of testing
  - Professional fees
  - Labour costs arising directly from construction or purchase of asset (IAS 16: para. 15 - 17)

Do **not** capitalise:

- Repair, maintenance and servicing costs
- Administrative and general overheads (IAS 16: para. 19)

Treatment of sales tax (VAT):

If business is VAT-registered:

- Do **not** include VAT in the cost of the asset (it is debited to the VAT control a/c instead & reclaimed from HMRC)

If business in not VAT-registered:

- Include VAT in the cost of the asset (it cannot be reclaimed from HMRC)

As non-current assets are often among the most expensive things a business purchases, the expenditure must be appropriately authorised to ensure:

- Assets are not bought unnecessarily
- Assets are acquired at the best prices and on the best terms

Level of authorisation depends on cost eg

- Low cost – supervisor
- Medium cost – manager
- High cost – business owner

Business will set thresholds

There are different ways of funding the purchase of non-current assets:

| Method | Explanation |
|---|---|
| Cash | Includes cash payments for non-current assets and purchases on standard commercial credit terms |
| Loan | A fixed amount borrowed from a bank or other provider to be repaid over an agreed period of time – interest is paid on the outstanding amount |
| Hire purchase | An initial deposit to the finance company followed by a fixed number of instalments after which the asset is legally owned |
| Finance lease | Similar to hire purchase but there is normally no option to purchase the asset at the end of the lease term |
| Part-exchange | An old asset is given as part payment for a new asset with the rest of the purchase price being paid in cash |

**Cash purchase:**

If business if VAT-registered and VAT is recoverable:

| | | | |
|---|---|---|---|
| DEBIT | Non-current asset at cost | £10,000 | |
| DEBIT | VAT control account | £2,000 | |
| CREDIT | Bank | | £12,000 |

If business if not VAT-registered:

| | | | |
|---|---|---|---|
| DEBIT | Non-current asset at cost | £12,000 | |
| CREDIT | Bank | | £12,000 |

**Financed by bank loan:**

When bank loan taken out:

| | | | |
|---|---|---|---|
| DEBIT | Bank | £12,000 | |
| CREDIT | Loan | | £12,000 |

Then the double entry for a cash purchase (as above) is required.

**Purchased under a hire purchase or finance lease agreement:**

Ignoring the effect of VAT (as unlikely to be tested for hire purchase/finance lease):

| | |
|---|---|
| DEBIT | Non-current asset at cost |
| CREDIT | Liability |

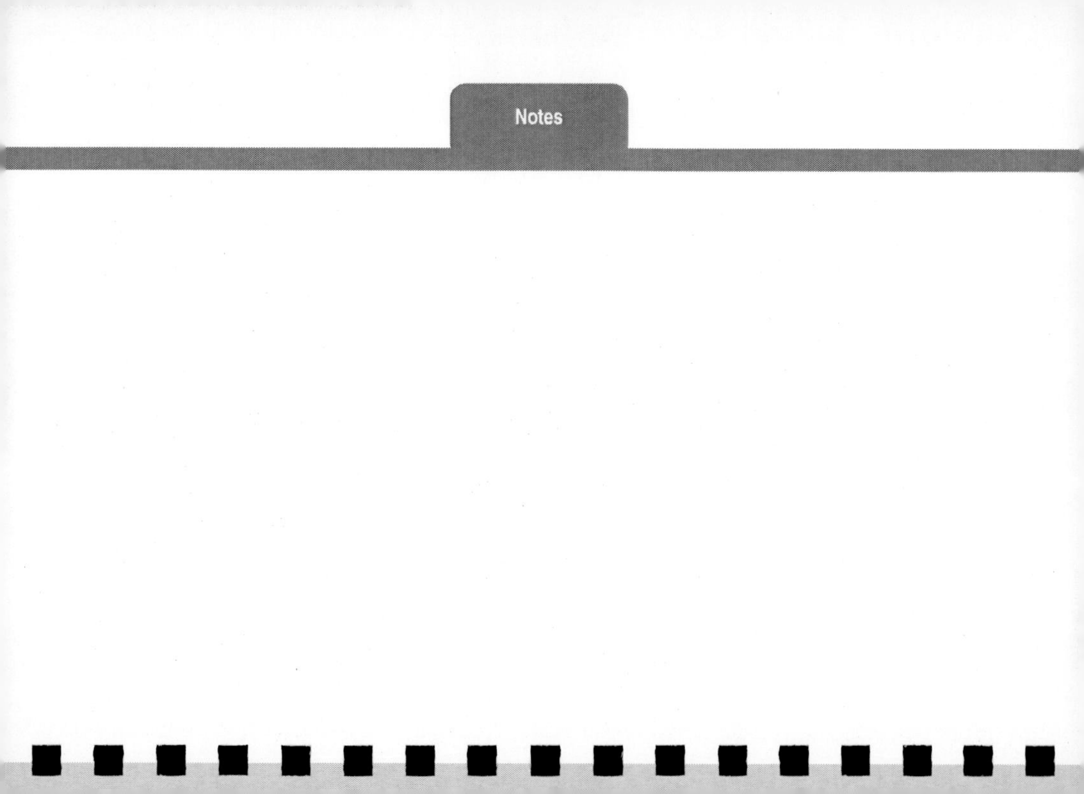
Notes

# 4: Depreciation of non-current assets

## Topic List

What is depreciation?

Depreciation methods

Assets acquired partway through year

Double entry

*The first two tasks of the assessment are likely to include calculation of depreciation for the year, entry of depreciation into the non-current asset register and recording depreciation in ledger accounts.*

## What is depreciation?

**Depreciation**: the measure of the cost of the economic benefits of the asset that have been consumed during the period

Depreciation is charged to allocate a fair proportion of the non-current asset's cost to the period benefiting from its use.

Carrying amount of asset = Cost − Accumulated depreciation

DEBIT → Statement of profit or loss → Depreciation charge for the year
CREDIT → Statement of financial position → Accumulated depreciation

## Straight line method

There are two ways of calculating straight line depreciation:

$$\text{Depreciation} = \frac{\text{Cost} - \text{Residual value}}{\text{Useful life (years)}}$$

or

(Cost – Residual value) × %

## Diminishing balance method

Depreciation

= Depreciation rate (%) × Carrying amount (cost – accumulated depreciation)

**Note.** This method does not take account of any residual value, since the carrying amount under this method will never reach zero.

# Units of production method

$$\text{Depreciation} = \frac{\text{Number of units produced}}{\text{Life in number of units}} \times (\text{Cost} - \text{Residual value})$$

| Options | Task instructions |
|---|---|
| **Either** to charge 12 months' worth of depreciation in the year of acquisition irrespective of when the asset was acquired. | Here the exam task may state that **'a full year's depreciation is applied in the year of acquisition'**. |
| **Or** to calculate depreciation on a **pro-rata** basis which means it will only charge depreciation on the asset for the **number of months it was held.** | Here the exam task is likely to say **'depreciation is calculated on an annual basis and charged in equal instalments for each full month an asset is owned in the year'**. |

This will not be tested for the diminishing balance method as the syllabus learning outcome is 'use the diminishing balance method of depreciation for a full year using a percentage'.

| | | |
|---|---|---|
| DEBIT | Depreciation charges (SPL) | £15,000 | |
| CREDIT | Non-current asset accumulated depreciation (SOFP) | | £15,000 |

Example of ledger accounts:

## Depreciation charges

| | £ | | £ |
|---|---|---|---|
| Accumulated depreciation | 6,000 | Profit or loss account | 6,000 |
| | | | |
| | 6,000 | | 6,000 |

## Accumulated depreciation

| | £ | | £ |
|---|---|---|---|
| Balance c/d | 24,000 | Balance b/d | 18,000 |
| | | Depreciation charges | 6,000 |
| | 24,000 | | 24,000 |

# 5: Disposal of non-current assets

## Topic List

Disposals

Part exchange

Non-current asset register

Reconciliation

*You need to know how to calculate the gain/loss on disposal and the accounting entries to record a disposal or part exchange. You are also likely to be asked to record a disposal in the non-current assets register and could be asked about the purpose and content of the non-current asset register.*

# Disposals

**1** Calculate the gain/loss on disposal

| | £ | £ |
|---|---|---|
| Sales proceeds | | X |
| Less cost of making the sale | | (X) |
| Net sales proceeds | | X |
| Cost of non-current asset | X | |
| Less accumulated depreciation | (X) | |
| Carrying amount | | (X) |
| Gain/(loss) on disposal | | X/(X) |

**2** The following must appear in the disposals account:

(a) Original cost of the asset (DR)

(b) Accumulated depreciation (CR)

(c) Net sales proceeds (CR)

**3** Ledger accounting entries:

(a) DEBIT Disposals
CREDIT Non-current asset at cost
*with cost of asset*

(b) DEBIT Accumulated depreciation
CREDIT Disposals
*with accumulated dep'n*

(c) DEBIT Bank
CREDIT Disposals
*with proceeds of asset sale*

**4** The balance on the disposal account is the gain/loss on disposal which is recorded in the profit or loss ledger account.

## Disposals

| | £ | | £ |
|---|---|---|---|
| Non-current asset cost | 200 | Accumulated depriciation | 100 |
| Profit or loss account | 30 | Bank | 130 |
| | ___ | | ___ |
| | 230 | | 230 |

**Alert!** Disposals are a key area. Make sure you can post the ledger entries correctly.

## Depreciation policy:

'A full year is charged in the year of acquisition and none in the year of disposal' – depreciation for year = 0

or

'Pro-rata basis' – only charge depreciation for months asset was held in year

# Part exchange

The part exchange allowance is part of the cost of the new asset and the disposal proceeds of the old asset.

The journals required are:

1. DEBIT Non-current asset at cost
   CREDIT Disposals
   *with the part exchange allowance*

2. DEBIT Non-current asset at cost
   CREDIT Bank
   *with the balance paid for the new asset*

Disposals, like acquisitions, need to be **authorised**.

This is a record of all the tangible non-current assets owned by the business and lists detailed information eg

- Item name/serial number
- Location
- Department responsible for asset
- Asset type
- Cost
- Funding method
- Acquisition date
- Depreciation policy
- Depreciation charges to date
- Carrying amount
- Disposal date
- Disposal proceeds

Method for assessment tasks:

1. Read requirements
2. Scan question and note the depreciation method(s)
3. Read information on any acquisitions and make postings (description, acquisition date, funding method)
4. Calculate and record depreciation on new asset(s)
5. Read information on any disposals and make postings (depreciation charges, carrying amount, disposal proceeds, disposal date)
6. Calculate and record depreciation on other non-current assets in register
7. Review your answer – does it make sense?

## Reconciling physical assets, ledger accounts and register

The non-current assets register must reconcile (agree) with both the general ledger and the assets themselves.

## Physical checks

- Check asset in register still exists in the business
- Check that each asset in the business is recorded in the register

## Discrepancies

Discrepancies have to be investigated.

- Asset in business not in register → when asset purchased no entries put in register
- Entries in register not up to date, eg depreciation charge not entered each year
- Asset in register but no physical asset → asset sold/scrapped/stolen and not recorded

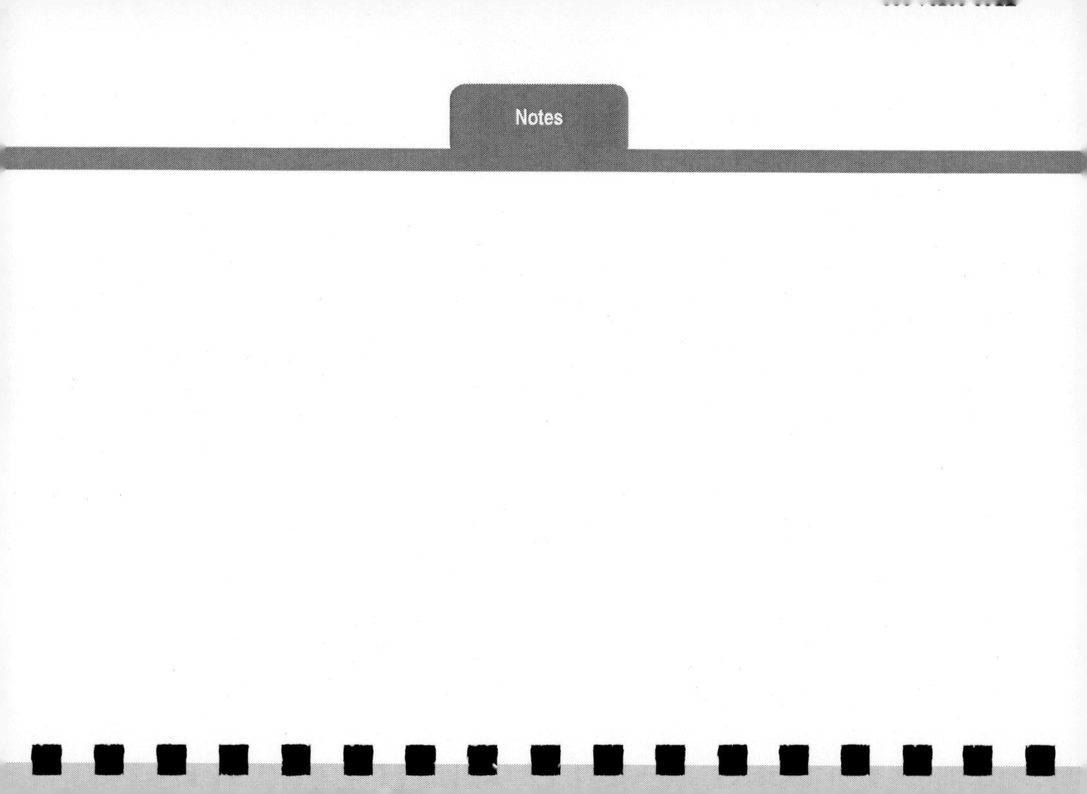

Notes

# 6: Accruals and prepayments

## Topic List

Accrued expenses

Prepaid expenses

Accrued and prepaid income

*Task 3 of your assessment is likely to focus on accruals and prepayments. Calculations, ledger accounting and completing sentences could be tested and the task could include ethical principles.*

# Accrued expenses

Where expenses have been incurred but not invoiced/paid for at the end of the accounting period

Expense incurred – no invoice yet

Part relating to current accounting period is an accrual (a liability in the SOFP).

We **debit** the expense account and **credit** the accrued expenses account (a current liability) in the SOFP. At the beginning of the next accounting period this accrual is reversed by crediting the expense account and debiting the accrued expenses account in the SOFP.

## Example

A business had an accrual for gas expenses of £200 at 31 March 20X3. You are accounting for gas expenses for the year ended 31 March 20X4. The cash book for the year shows payments for gas expenses of £3,500. On 3 June 20X4, the business receives a bill for £900 for the 3 months to 31 May 20X4. £900 × 1/3 = accrual of £300.

**Gas expenses (SPL)**

| | £ | | £ |
|---|---|---|---|
| Bank | 3,500 | Accrued expenses (reversal) | 200 |
| Accrued expenses | 300 | Profit or loss a/c | 3,600 |
| | 3,800 | | 3,800 |

**Accrued expenses (SOFP)**

| | £ | | £ |
|---|---|---|---|
| Gas expenses | 200 | Balance b/d | 200 |
| Balance c/d | 300 | Gas expenses | 300 |
| | 500 | | 500 |
| | | Balance b/d | 300 |

# Prepaid expenses

When an expense has been paid in the accounting period but it relates to the following accounting period.

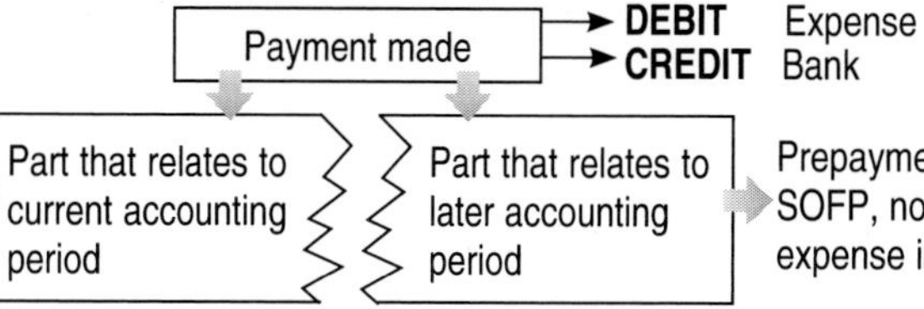


Prepayment. An asset in the SOFP, not charged as an expense in SPL

We **credit** the expense with the amount prepaid thereby reducing the expense and **debit** prepaid expenses (a current asset) in the SOFP. At the beginning of the following accounting period, the prepayment is reversed by debiting the expense and crediting prepaid expenses.

## Example

You are accounting for insurance expenses for the year ended 31 December 20X4. At 31 December 20X3, there was a prepayment for insurance expenses of £250. The cash book for the year shows payments for insurance expenses of £1,500. This amount is for insurance for the year to 31 March 20X5. Prepayment = £1,500 × 3/12 = £375.

**Insurance expenses (SPL)**

| | £ | | £ |
|---|---|---|---|
| Prepaid expenses (reversal) | 250 | Prepaid expenses | 375 |
| Bank | 1,500 | Profit or loss a/c | 1,375 |
| | 1,750 | | 1,750 |

**Prepaid expenses (SOFP)**

| | £ | | £ |
|---|---|---|---|
| Balance b/d | 250 | Insurance expenses | 250 |
| Insurance expenses | 375 | Balance b/d | 375 |
| | 625 | | 625 |
| Balance b/d | 375 | | |

## Prepaid income

When sundry income (eg rent) is received which relates to the following accounting period.

Proportion of income relating to future periods is removed from income in the SPL and a corresponding current liability (prepaid income) is recognised in the SOFP.

| | |
|---|---|
| DEBIT | Income (SPL) |
| CREDIT | Prepaid income (SOFP) = current liability |

At the beginning of the following accounting period, the b/d prepaid income balance needs to be reversed:

| | |
|---|---|
| DEBIT | Prepaid income (SOFP) |
| CREDIT | Income |

## Accrued income

Where sundry income (eg interest receivable, commissions) has been earned but not received/invoiced.

Income earned in accounting period is added to income in the SPL and a corresponding current asset (accrued income) is recognised in the SOFP.

| | |
|---|---|
| DEBIT | Accrued income (SOFP) = current asset |
| CREDIT | Income (SPL) |

At the beginnning of the following accounting period, the b/d accrued income balance needs to be reversed:

| | |
|---|---|
| DEBIT | Income (SPL) |
| CREDIT | Accrued income (SOFP) |

Notes

# 7: Inventories

## Topic List

Physical count of inventory

Valuation of inventory

Accounting for inventory

*This is an important chapter. It covers inventory, which is a key figure in both the statement of profit or loss and the statement of financial position.*

## Overview of inventory

Under the accruals concept only the cost of goods sold in the period should be charged to the statement of profit or loss. An adjustment is made at the year end to reflect the value in inventory.

### End of year procedures

- Physically count the inventory
- Value the inventory
- Adjust the ledger accounts to reflect the value of closing inventory

## Physical count of inventory

### Physical count

At the end of the accounting period each item of inventory is physically counted and listed.

### Inventory records

Records quantity purchased for each delivery, quantity issued for sale/processing and the quantity on hand

### Reconciliation

Quantity counted is compared to the inventory records. All discrepancies must be investigated.

- Errors in recording deliveries/issues
- Stolen items
- Damaged items
- Inventory sold but not yet despatched

## Value of closing inventory

Quantity of inventory × Value per item = Value of inventory

## Rule for valuing inventory (IAS 2)

Inventory is valued at the **lower** of:

- Cost and
- Net realisable value (IAS 2: para. 6)

## Cost

- IAS 2 – all costs of purchase, costs of conversion and other costs incurred in bringing the items to their present location and condition (IAS 2: para. 10)

**Note.** Exclude storage costs of finished goods and selling costs (IAS 2: para. 16)

## Net realisable value (NRV)

The expected selling price of the inventory, less any further costs to be incurred such as estimated costs of completion and selling/distribution costs (IAS 2: para. 6)

# Methods of determining cost

Where deliveries and issues of inventory are made on a regular basis, it is impossible, in practice, to determine precisely which items have been sold and which remain in inventory at the year end. The cost of inventory is therefore determined using one of the following methods.

## First in, First out (FIFO)

Assumes:

- Items issued/sold are the earliest purchases
- Inventory comprises the most recent purchases (IAS 2: para. 27)

## Last in, First out (LIFO)

Assumes:

- Items issued/sold are the most recent purchases
- Inventory comprises the earliest purchases
- NB LIFO is not permitted under IAS 2

## Weighted average cost (AVCO)

- After each purchase a weighted average cost per item is calculated:

$$\frac{\text{Total cost of items held}}{\text{Number of units held}}$$

- Inventory is valued at the average cost at the end of the year (IAS 2: para. 27)

# Calculating the cost of inventory from the selling price

If business is registered for VAT:

| | |
|---|---|
| Sales price (net of VAT) | X * |
| Less: Profit | (X) |
| Cost | X |

* Sales price gross of VAT × 100/120

***Note.*** *VAT is deducted from the sales price as it does not belong to the business – the business is collecting the sales tax on behalf of HMRC*

If business is not registered for VAT:

| | |
|---|---|
| Sales price | X * |
| Less: Profit | (X) |
| Cost | X |

* As the business is not registered for VAT, it will not charge its customers VAT so there will be no VAT included in the sales price

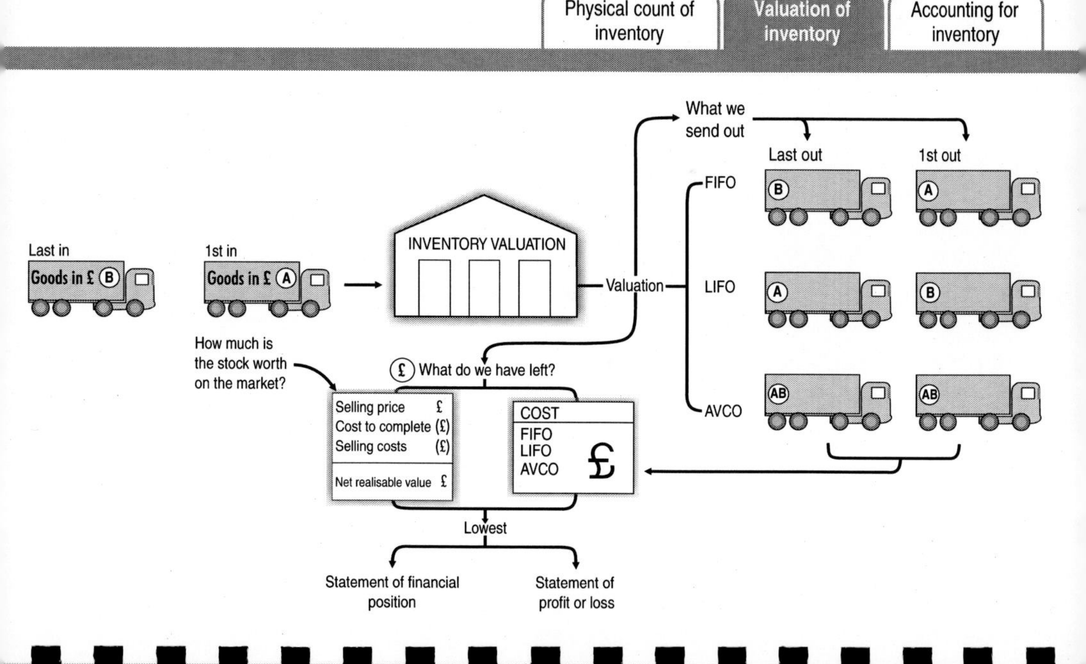
Last in
Goods in £ B
1st in
Goods in £ A
INVENTORY VALUATION
Valuation
What we send out
Last out
1st out
FIFO
LIFO
AVCO
How much is the stock worth on the market?
£ What do we have left?
Selling price £
Cost to complete (£)
Selling costs (£)
Net realisable value £
COST
FIFO
LIFO
AVCO
£
Lowest
Statement of financial position
Statement of profit or loss

| | |
|---|---|
| Opening inventory | X |
| Purchases | X |
| Less: Closing inventory | (X) |
| | X |

**During the year:**

DEBIT Purchases
CREDIT Bank/purchases ledger control account

**At the year end:**

DEBIT Closing inventory – statement of financial position

CREDIT Closing inventory – statement of profit or loss

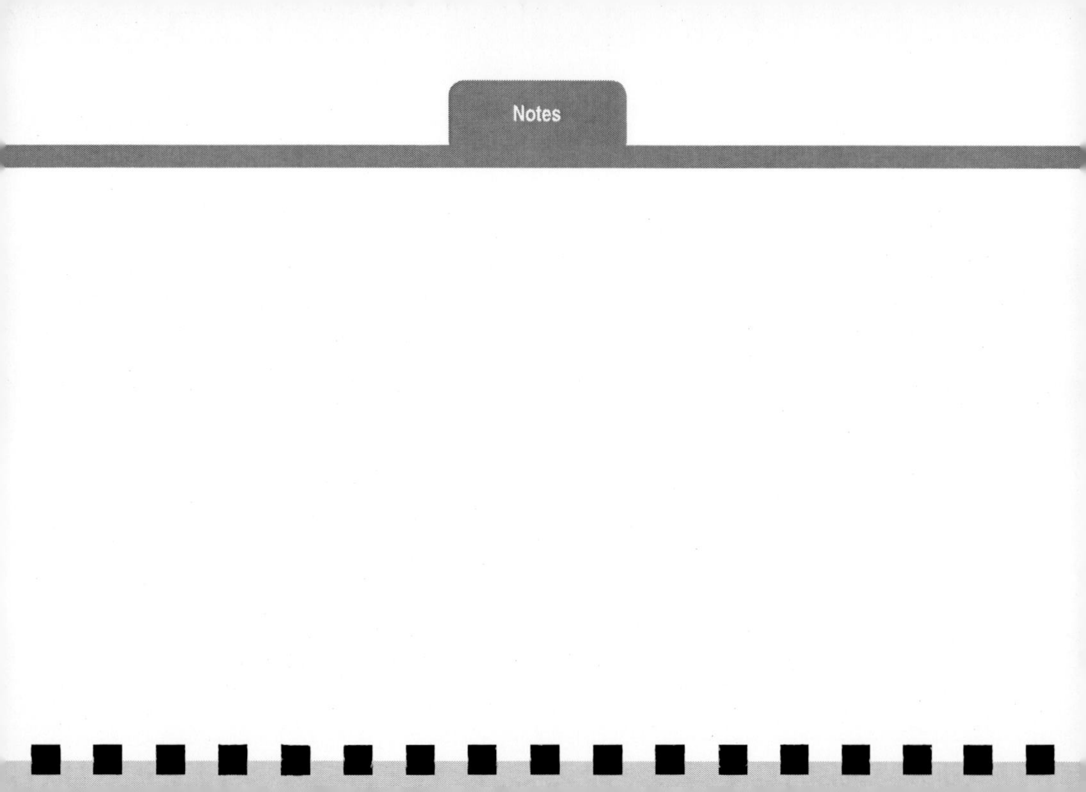
Notes

# 8: Irrecoverable and doubtful debts

## Topic List

Irrecoverable debts and doubtful debts

Recovery of debts

*Irrecoverable debts and doubtful debts are considered at the end of the accounting period. Irrecoverable debts may require writing out of the accounts and doubtful debts should have an allowance made against them.*

# Irrecoverable debts and doubtful debts

Under the prudence concept a receivable should only be classed as an asset if it is recoverable.

## Irrecoverable debts

If definitely irrecoverable, it should be written off as an irrecoverable debts expense.

DEBIT Irrecoverable debts (SPL)
CREDIT Sales ledger control account (SOFP)

The customer's individual account in the sales ledger is also credited to remove the debt.

## Doubtful debts

If uncertainty exists as to the recoverability of the debt, prudence dictates that an allowance for doubtful debts should be set up. This allowance is offset against the receivables balance in the statement of financial position (accruals concept).

DEBIT Allowance for doubtful debts – adjustments (SPL)

CREDIT Allowance for doubtful debts (SOFP)

The allowance for doubtful debts can either be specific, against a particular receivable, or general, against a proportion of all receivables that are not specifically allowed for.

When calculating a general allowance for doubtful debts to be made, the following order applies:

| | | £ |
|---|---|---|
| Receivables balance per SLCA | | X |
| Less: | irrecoverable debts written off | (X) |
| | debts with a specific allowance | (X) |
| Balance on which general allowance is calculated | | X |

**Note.** Only the **movement** in the allowance (including both general and specific amount) needs to be accounted for.

| | £ |
|---|---|
| Allowance required at year end | X |
| Existing allowance (general and specific) | (X) |
| Increase/(decrease) required | X/(X) |

## Accounting entries

| | | DEBIT | CREDIT |
|---|---|---|---|
| (1) | Write off irrecoverable debts | Irrecoverable debts (SPL) | Sales ledger control account (SOFP) |
| (2) | Set up allowance | Allowance for doubtful debts – adjustments (SPL) | Allowance for doubtful debts (SOFP) |
| (3) | Increase allowance | Allowance for doubtful debts – adjustments (SPL) | Allowance for doubtful debts (SOFP) |
| (4) | Reduce allowance | Allowance for doubtful debts (SOFP) | Allowance for doubtful debts – adjustments (SPL) |

## Subsequent recovery of debts written off

If a debt is recovered, having previously been written off in a previous period as irrecoverable, then:

DEBIT Bank
CREDIT Irrecoverable debts (SPL)

# 9: Bank reconciliations

## Topic List



*This is an important chapter. The bank reconciliation is a key means of control of one of business's key assets, cash held at the bank. It is very likely that this topic will be tested in your assessment.*

## Purpose of reconciliations

- To identify errors – made either by the business in writing up the books or by the bank in maintaining the account
- To identify omissions eg bank charges, dishonoured cheques, standing orders, direct debits and interest
- To identify timing differences eg unrecorded lodgements, unpresented cheques
- To verify the accuracy of the bank balance in the year end financial statements

## Checking the bank statement to the cash book

**STEP 1** Tick all of the receipts on the bank statement to the entries in the debit side of the cash book

**STEP 2** Tick all of the payments on the bank statement to the entries in the credit side of the cash book

**STEP 3** Check any unticked items on the bank statement to ensure the bank has not made a mistake

**STEP 4** Make any necessary adjustments to the cash book and general ledger to record any legitimate unticked items on the bank statement

## Examples of cash book adjustments

- BACS direct credit from a customer not recorded in the cash book
- Bank charges not entered in the cash book
- The amount of a cheque incorrectly recorded in the cash book
- A cheque from a customer dishonoured by the bank

**Alert! Remember that the bank statement and the cash book are mirror images of each other, ie a debit entry in the cash book is a credit on the bank statement**

- After correcting the cash book for legitimate differences from the bank statement, we can calculate the adjusted balance in the cash book
- We can now produce the bank reconciliation statement – any unticked items in the cash book are due to **timing differences**

## Bank reconciliation statement

| | £ |
|---|---|
| Balance per bank statement | X |
| Plus: Unrecorded lodgements | X |
| Less: Unpresented cheques | (X) |
| Balance as per corrected cash book | X |

## Timing differences

**Unrecorded lodgements**
Cash/cheques from customers paid into the bank and recorded in the cash book, which do not appear on the bank statement due to the delay caused by the clearing system

**Unpresented cheques**
Cheques to suppliers entered in the cash book, which do not appear on the bank statement as they have not yet been either banked by the supplier or cleared by the bank

# Bank reconciliations - approach to assessment tasks

1. Set up two columns – 'cash book adjustments' and 'bank statement – timing differences'
2. Read scenario and enter opening balances at the top of each column
3. For each item in scenario, determine whether it:
   - Affects the cash book or bank statement
   - Increases or decreases that balance

   Note the correct treatment in the appropriate column
4. Total both columns and if you have posted the adjustments correctly, the adjusted balances should reconcile
5. To answer the task requirement, ensure that the relevant items are included in your on-screen solution

# 10: Control account reconciliations

## Topic List



*In this chapter we consider the reconcilations that are prepared for the sales ledger and purchases ledger control accounts with the sales and purchases ledgers respectively. You must be able to perform the reconciliations and process any adjustments required.*

## Basic accounting system for sales on credit

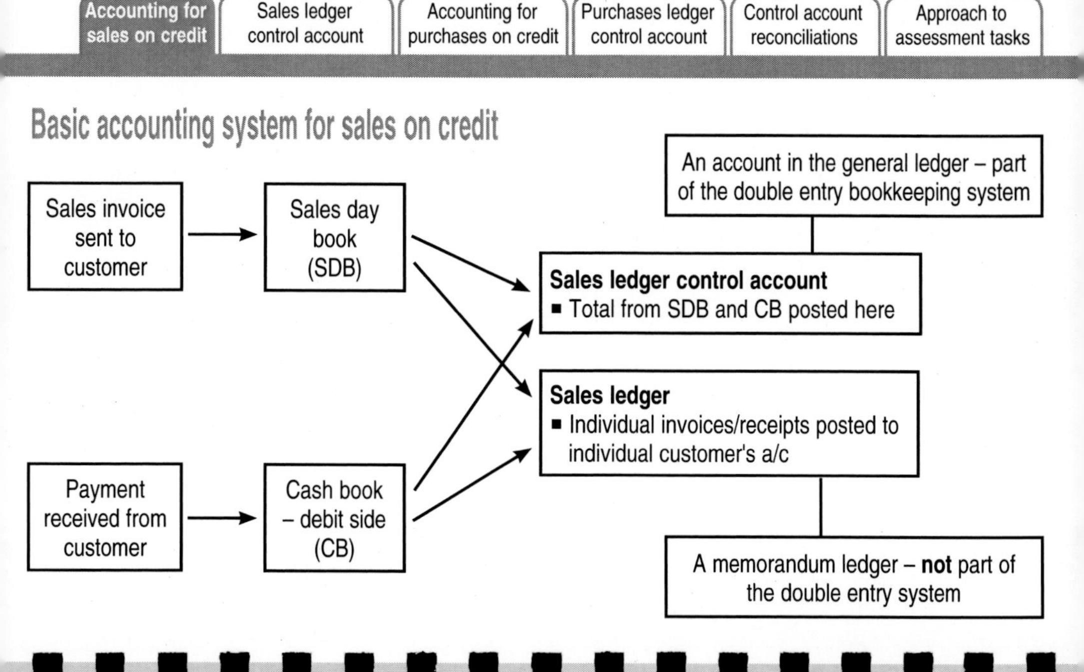

# Sales ledger control account

As well as the basic entries for invoices and cash, the control account will contain other entries for items such as discounts allowed, debts written off, etc.

**Sales ledger control account (SLCA)**

| | £ | | £ |
|---|---|---|---|
| Balance b/d | X | Sales returns | X |
| Credit sales | X | Receipts from customers | X |
| Dishonoured cheques | X | Discounts allowed | X |
| | | Irrecoverable debts written off | X |
| | | Contra entry with PLCA | X |
| | _ | Balance c/d | X |
| | X | | X |
| Balance b/d | X | | |

**Source**

- Dishonoured cheques – bank returns customer's cheque unpaid – Debit SLCA, Credit Bank
- Sales returns – from sales returns day book
- Discounts allowed – from discounts allowed day book
- Contra entry (set off) – an amount owing by a customer which is set off against the amount owed by the business to them as a supplier. The other side of the entry is in the purchases ledger control account.

## Basic accounting system for purchases on credit

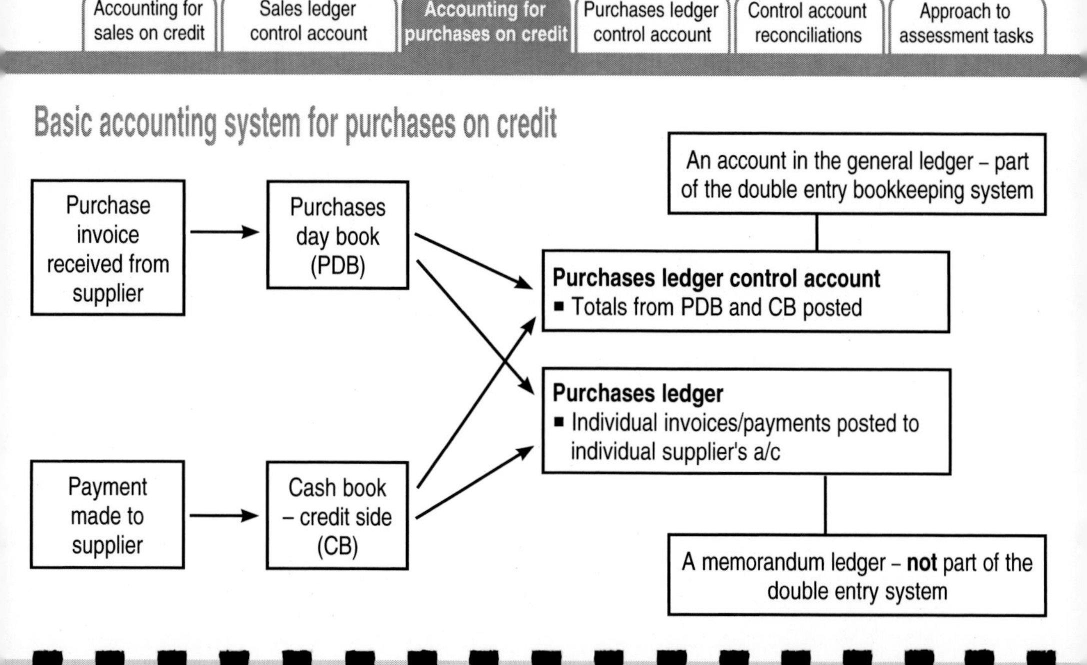

# Purchases ledger control account

As well as the basic entries for invoices and cash the control account will contain other entries for items such as discounts received, purchases returned, etc.

**Purchases ledger control account (PLCA)**

| | £ | | £ |
|---|---|---|---|
| Purchases returns | X | Balance b/d | X |
| Payments to suppliers | X | Credit purchases | X |
| Discounts received | X | | |
| Contra entry with SLCA | X | | |
| Balance c/d | X | | _ |
| | X | | X |
| | | Balance b/d | X |

**Source**

- Purchases returns – from purchases returns day book
- Discounts received – from discounts received day book
- Contra entry (set off) – an amount owed to a supplier which is set off against the amount owed by the supplier as a credit customer. The other side of the entry is in the sales ledger control account.

Balance on the control account — Should = — Total of balances in the memorandum ledger

SLCA = Receivables in statement of financial position

PLCA = Payables in statement of financial position

## Purpose of control account reconciliation

- To **verify the accuracy** of the receivables and payables figures in the year end financial statements
- To identify **errors and omissions** made by the business in writing up the books

## The reconciliation

- A comparision of the balance on the control account with the total of the list of the balances from the memorandum ledger, to check for errors and omissions
- All errors and omissions must be noted and appropriate adjustments made to the accounts via the journal

**Examples of errors affecting the control account**

- Books of prime entry under- or over-cast
- Postings from books of prime entry made to wrong side of control account
- Discounts incorrectly treated in the control account
- Irrecoverable debts/contras not entered in the control account

**Examples of errors affecting the memorandum ledger**

- Transaction in book of prime entry entered in wrong account
- Postings from books of prime entry made to wrong side of the memorandum ledger
- Entry from books of prime entry posted as wrong amount in the memorandum ledger

| Example of error | Adjustment required to control a/c or memorandum ledger |
|---|---|
| Page of cash receipts book undercast by £500 | CR SLCA £500 |
| Irrecoverable debt of £800 written off in customer account but not in SLCA | CR SLCA £800 |
| Cash receipt entered into customer's account as £150 instead of £510 | CR Sales ledger £360 |
| Purchases day book overcast by £1,000 | DR PLCA £1,000 |
| Purchase invoice entered into supplier's account as £450 instead of £540 | CR Purchases ledger £90 |
| Discounts received of £850 credited to the PLCA | DR PLCA £1,700 (£850 × 2) |

# Control account reconciliations - approach to assessment tasks

1. Set up 2 columns – 'control account' and 'memorandum ledger total'
2. Read scenario and enter opening balances at the top of each column
3. For each error in scenario, determine whether it:
   - affects the control account or memorandum ledger
   - increases or decreases that balance

   Note the correct treatment in the appropriate column
4. Total both columns and if you have posted the adjustments correctly, the adjusted balances should reconcile
5. To answer the task requirement, ensure that the relevant adjustments are included in your on-screen solution

# 11: The trial balance, errors and the suspense account

## Topic List



*In this chapter we revise the types of error that may occur in accounts and whether these cause a suspense account to be created in the trial balance. We also look at clearing the suspense account and preparing a trial balance. The assessment will include tasks testing the preparation of a trial balance and the correction of errors in the trial balance.*

## Trial balance

A **trial balance** is a list of ledger balances shown in debit and credit columns.

The debits should equal the credits.

If the trial balance does not balance, you need to set up a suspense account.

## Suspense account

This is a **temporary** account set up to make the trial balance balance. Errors need to be found and corrected, clearing the suspense account, before the financial statements are prepared.

## Errors which allow the trial balance to balance

| Type of error | Detail |
|---|---|
| Error of omission | Both sides of a transaction have been completely left out eg a rent payment of £800 is not recorded in the general ledger. |
| Error of original entry | Debits = credits but the amount is incorrect eg a credit sale of £1,000 is posted as:<br>DEBIT Sales ledger control account £150<br>CREDIT Sales £150 |
| Reversal of entries | Transaction is recorded at correct amount but debit and credit entries have been reversed eg posting the credit sale above as:<br>DEBIT Sales £1,000<br>CREDIT Sales ledger control account £1,000 |

## Errors which allow the trial balance to balance

| Type of error | Detail |
|---|---|
| Error of principle | Debits = credits but one of the entries has been made to the wrong type of account eg £500 spent on repairing a motor vehicle has been recorded as:<br>DEBIT Motor vehicles at cost £500<br>CREDIT Bank £500 |
| Error of commission | Debits = credits but one of the entries has been made to the wrong account, but not the wrong type of account eg £200 spent on telephone costs has been recorded as:<br>DEBIT Insurance expense £200<br>CREDIT Bank £200 |

## Errors resulting on an imbalance in the trial balance (TB)

- One-sided entry
- Entry duplicated on one side, nothing on the other
- Unequal entries eg transposition error
- Balance incorrectly transferred to TB
- Balance omitted from the TB

→

- Result in the creation of a suspense account on the TB
- Correction of the errors will clear the suspense account

| Type of error | Adjustment required |
|---|---|
| One-sided entry eg debit made in ledger but not the credit entry | Make the missing entry (credit) and post the other side (debit) to the suspense account (a/c) |
| Entry duplicated on one side, nothing on the other eg cash sale recorded as DR Bank £400 DR Sales £400 | Post the a/c that was posted on the wrong side with twice the amount on the correct side (CR Sales £800) and post the other side to the suspense a/c (DR Suspense £800) |
| Unequal entries eg £10 debited to purchases (correct amount £100), £100 credited to bank | In the a/c with the wrong posting, post an amount to correct it and post the other side to the suspense a/c. eg DR Purchases £90, CR Suspense £90 |
| Balance incorrectly transferred to TB eg Bank debit balance of £10,000 written into TB as £1,000 debit | In the a/c with the wrong balance, post an amount to correct the balance and post the other side to the suspense a/c. eg DR Bank £9,000, CR Suspense £9,000 |
| Balance omitted from TB eg selling expenses of £2,500 | Enter the missing balance (selling expenses as a debit of £2,500) and post the amount on the other side in the suspense a/c (CR Suspense £2,500) |

## Journal

The journal records transactions **not covered by other books of original entry**.

Journals can be used to correct errors. The journal **must** have a **debit equal** in value **to the credit**.

The format of a journal entry is:

| Date | Reference | £ | £ |
|---|---|---|---|
| | Account to be debited | X | |
| | Account to be credited | | X |

*Narrative to explain the transaction*

**Alert!** You may be asked for the journal entry of a transaction in an assessment.

## Year end adjustments

Journals are also used to process year end adjustments such as

- Depreciation charges
- Accruals and prepayments
- Irrecoverable debts and doubtful debts
- Closing inventory

## Period end considerations

Be aware that period end adjustments can have an:

- Effect on profit
- Effect on assets and liabilities
- Impact on management performance
- Impact on stakeholder decisions based on company performance

Errors and omissions may arise because of:

- Mistakes
- Time pressure at period end
- Poor management decisions
- Failure to follow guidance or regulations
- Deliberate manipulation
- Pressure from management to achieve a certain result

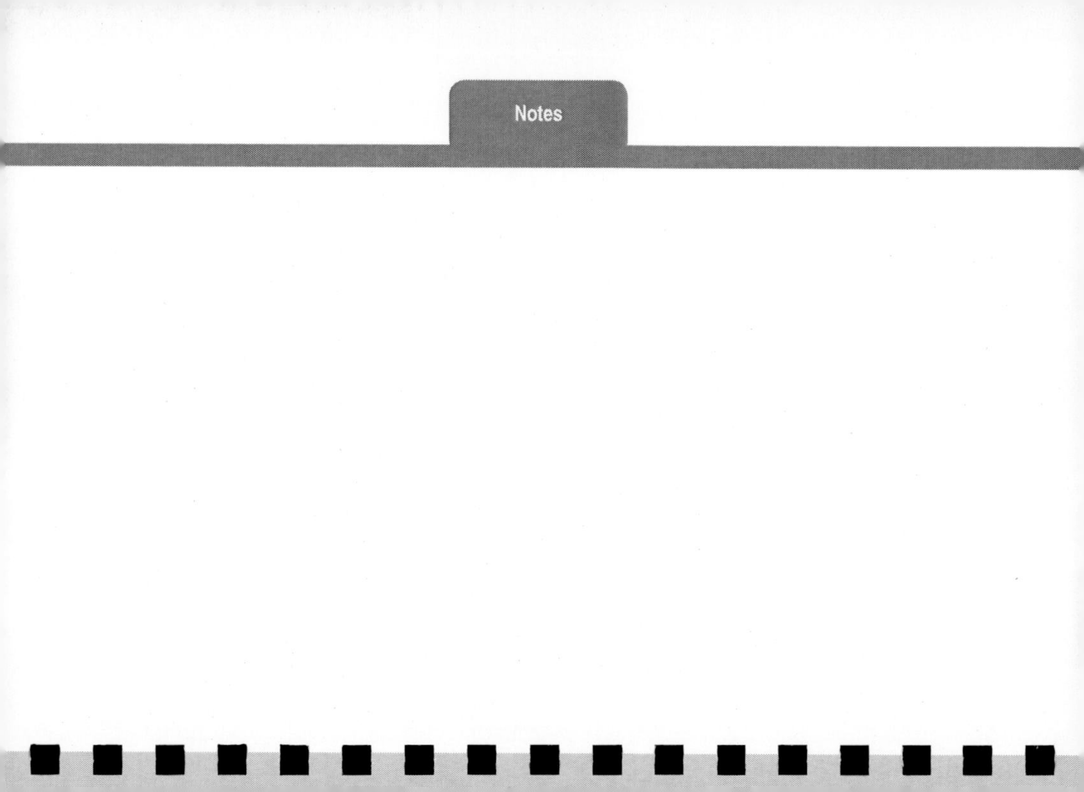

Notes

# 12: The extended trial balance

## Topic List



*You will usually be given tasks involving an extended trial balance (ETB) in your assessment. You must understand the layout of the ETB, know how to process adjustments through the ETB and then extend each line in the appropriate statement of profit or loss or statement of financial position column.*

**Extended trial balance (ETB)**: a technique that allows the initial trial balance to be adjusted for any errors or year end adjustments; it is then used as the basis for the preparation of the financial statements

The ETB headings are:

| *Ledger account* | *Ledger balance* | | *Adjustments* | | *Statement of profit or loss* | | *Statement of financial position* | |
|---|---|---|---|---|---|---|---|---|
| | DR | CR | DR | CR | DR | CR | DR | CR |
| | £ | £ | £ | £ | £ | £ | £ | £ |

# Preparing the ETB

1. Enter each ledger a/c balance as either a debit or credit in the ledger balance column. If debits don't equal credits, check the additions are correct, then insert a suspense account.

2. If there is a suspense account, deal with the errors that have caused this. Enter the adjustments in the Adjustments columns. Check that the suspense a/c has been cleared by your adjustments.

3. Make any year end adjustments:
   - Depreciation
   - Accruals and prepayments
   - Closing inventory
   - Irrecoverable and doubtful debts
   - Correction of errors/emissions

   You may need to enter some new account lines in the ETB.

4. Add the adjustments columns. Check the entries are correct and debits equal credits.

5. Add the figures across each line of the ETB and record total in SPL or SOFP as appropriate.

**6** Add the statement of profit or loss debits and credits to find the profit or loss for the year.

Take the profit or loss for the year to the statement of financial position columns:

- Profit = DEBIT SPL = CREDIT SFP
- Loss = CREDIT SPL = DEBIT SFP

**7** Add up the debits and credits in the statement of financial position and ensure they are equal.

**Alert! Remember**

**Statement of profit or loss**
- Income
- Expenses

**Statement of financial position**
- Assets
- Liabilities
- Capital

**Opening inventory is a debit to the statement of profit or loss (SPL)**

Notes

Notes